D059115

Rejoice!
Poetry Celebrating Life in the Amazon Rainf

Written and illustrated by the third grade students of Mendon Center Elementary in Pittsford, NY

ORIGINAL COVER

Introduction

The Amazon Rainforest in South America is the Earth's largest rainforest. In the rainforest, the temperatures are very hot, and it rains an average of 100 inches a year. Sometimes it can rain as much as 240 inches in a year! The rainforest has many layers and thousands of different species living in those layers. In fact, at least half of the species on Earth live in tropical rainforests. There is a lot of life to celebrate!

The Amazon Rainforest, however, is in trouble. Trees are being cut down for their valuable wood and to clear the land for farming and building. When the rainforest is cut down, the species living there are in danger of losing their habitat and becoming extinct. Also, because roughly 30 percent of the world's oxygen comes from the rainforest, there is not as much oxygen in the air to absorb carbon dioxide, a dangerous gas. The rainforest is disappearing so fast that by the year 2050, if nothing is done about it, it could be gone forever.

Meet the Authors

Front Row (left to right): Camber Hortop, Marisa Modugno, Jillian Gerhold, Emma Saubermann, Hannah Washburn, Christopher Downey, Kenny Mogauro, Ethan Medwetsky

Middle Row (left to right): Keith Mummery, Riley Leipold, Katie Forth, Sarah Garber, Flynn Herron, Liam Wilmot, Jack Rohrer, Eric Byington

Back Row (left to right): Mrs. Heather Clayton Kwit, Madeline Hobika, Matthew King, Jared Petrichick, Margaret Brennan, Jack Thornton, George Gines, Jack Romanick, Camille D'Arcy, Mrs. Kerin McKenna-Hussey, Mr. Adam Gursslin

Howl at Dawn

AHHOOOOOOOOOOOOOOO!
The howler's howl
Fills the morning air.
Birds flee from their perches
In the treetops.
Whoosh!
Branch to branch
He swings.
AHHOOOOOOOOOO!

It is dawn.

Water Rodents

Capybaras lumbering along—
Webbed feet,
Square snouts,
Short legs—
Perfect for them.
Quick treat of
Fruit and grass,
Then off to the water
For a swim and short nap.

Giant Amazon Water Lily

The river snakes on the forest
    floor.
Gracefully floating into view,
A giant green bottle cap.

Drifting

The water ripples slightly,
A small wave pushes it,
Out...
Of...
Sight....

6

Camouflage Critter

HISSSSSSSSSSSSSSSSSSSSSS
High up in the kapok tree
The tree boa lies
Twisted and dangling
A slender vine
With emerald green skin
And slick eyes
HISSSSSSSSSSSSSSSSSSSSSS

The Ants Go Marching

Clomp! Clomp! Clomp!
Hooked claws
Two antennae
Rough skin
Big compound eyes
Brown with a bit of black
Clomp! Clomp! Clomp!
Is there any insect more
Powerful than an army ant?

Butterfly Dancer

I dance on the treetops,
In the sun's spotlight,
Performing for the audience
    below.
The sun shines through
My papery wings—
A stained glass window.

Crafty Monkey

The capuchin
Genius—
Stealing fruit, slurping juice,
Waiting to get the nut.
Clever and cunning
Capuchin.

Fierce Feline

He's black and gold,
With dark coal spots
And stocky body,
Creeping through the forest
On strong legs for climbing.
Fast as the wind—
Purrrr, Purrrr

Liana's Strong Hold

Her ropy body
Quietly hugs the tree,
Making a spiral staircase.
The tree struggles to get away,
But can't do anything about it.
Swirling up and down the tree,
She reaches out to the next.
The liana makes a rainforest
    jungle gym
For the animals' swinging
    routines.

Shredders

Razor-sharp teeth
Snap! Snap!
The piranha sees prey
Snap! Snap!
The group shreds and bites,
Until their prey disappears.
They swim off in search
    of more.

Hairy Hunter

I creep
Along the wet, soggy ground.
I dig
A deep, dark burrow.
I hunt
During nightfall.
I sleep
A long sleep until my next
    meal.
Will I need a new burrow
Or just stay until sunlight?

The Harpy

Fierce, powerful harpy eagle
Soars down to catch prey.
Hooked talons and sharp beak—
    Not one monkey stands a
    chance
Against this monster of a bird.

Miniature Monkey

Small, small, small,
Swinging from tree to tree;
Skimming the canopy's
 surface
Eating bugs and fruit
Surprisingly big for him.

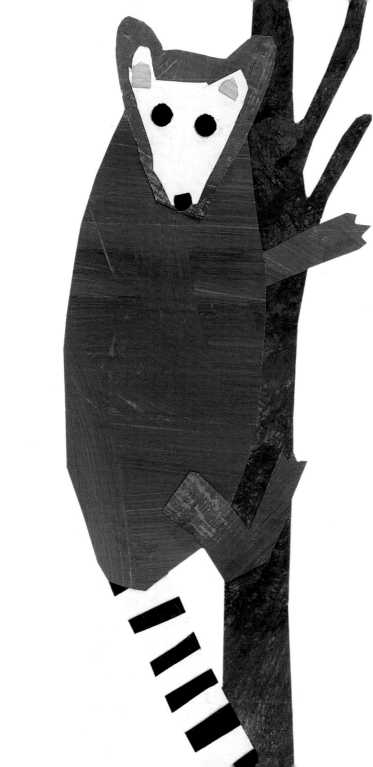

Coatimundi

Shh!
Shh!
Hear that?
It's a little beast
With canine teeth.
It has sharp claws
For climbing up trees,
And a striped tail
Signaling quietly to others.
Predator, predator—
Is that what it is saying?

The High Life

I am an epiphyte,
Growing on trees and other plants,
Soaking up moisture from the air,
Living without the soil below.
My sweet perfume attracts
    insects
For pollination.
My seeds drop and
Then an orchid appears.

Gems of the Rainforest

Gems of the rainforest,
Bright and poisonous,
Hopping around on the forest
    floor,
Carrying tadpoles to water
    ahead.
Does the predator dare to
    come near?

Katy-did, Katy-didn't

The dark night sky falls
Around these walking leaves.
The piano inside them plays
A beautiful rhythm:
"Katy-did, Katy-didn't!

Majestic Bird

A bold fruit tree stands in the
forest.
Suddenly,
SWOOP! Swish! SWOOP!
The toucan lands on a branch.
His black feathers shine.
He opens his banana bill—
Pluck! Gulp! Yum!

Escape Artist

I swing on the vines,
And I dash through the trees.
I escape the villainous harpy
    eagle
That may snatch me at any
    moment
As it hunts just above me.
But it cannot catch me,
For I am the spider monkey.

Sluggish Sloth

Sloooooooooooooooooow
Wet, lazy mammal
Wearing an algae coat
Infested with bugs.
He creeps through
the forest,
Unaware of what
Frightening animal
Might be lurking in the trees.

Bug Eaters

These plants are robbers;
They should be brought to
    justice.
The rainforest is their hideout—
Too bad
It's only the bugs
That can smell them out.

Scaly Skin

Dark skin, shocking green eyes,
Sharp, razor teeth.
Slithering in the damp mud,
Sleeping on the river bank,
He hides and then seeks his food.
Camouflaging in the plants,
A bumpy log.
He sees everything that comes by.
Be careful, he's not man's best
    friend.
He's the caiman.

Tamarins

He swings through
The trees
On long green ropes.
He flies through
The forest
On slick strips of green,
Hunting
For dinner.
So he searches
In a nearby
Bromeliad.

Predators

Hop! Hop!
A red-eyed tree frog
Hops from leaf to leaf.
He grips
With the help of
Sticky foot pads.

Boa watches carefully—
But bulging red eyes
Scare boa away.

Frog hops onto
Another leaf.
Crunch! Crunch!
Munch! Munch!
He gulps down a moth.
Safe for now.

About the Poems

HOWL AT DAWN

Howler monkeys give a howl every dawn in the rainforest. Their howls can be used to give warnings to other howler monkeys. However, howler monkeys don't howl at their enemies; they roar at them.

WATER RODENTS

Capybaras are the largest rodents in the world. They have webbed feet that make them great swimmers. If capybaras are swimming and get tired, they put their heads on the water line and fall asleep.

GIANT AMAZON WATER LILY

In the Amazon Rainforest, you can find giant plants. The Victoria Water Lily lives there, and it can grow as large as 8 feet wide and hold 300 pounds of weight. Its rims alone are 3 to 6 inches tall!

CAMOUFLAGE CRITTER

Emerald tree boas disguise as vines, and their prey can't see them because they blend into the trees so well. When emerald tree boas are in danger, they scare off their enemies by making a loud hissing sound.

THE ANTS GO MARCHING

The army ant sleeps in a ball with other ants. In the center of the ball are the queen ant and her babies. The ants cling together in a ball in order to protect the queen and her babies.

BUTTERFLY DANCER

The blue morpho butterfly is one of the biggest butterflies in the world. Its wingspan is 6 inches wide. Being big makes it easy to see, but when its wings are closed, it looks like a dead leaf.

CRAFTY MONKEY

Capuchin monkeys are very smart. They will pick ripe fruit, bite off the tip and drink the juice, and then leave the fruit with the nut inside. Later, when the fruit is hard, they gather it up, put it on a flat boulder, and crack it open to eat the nut inside. Capuchins will even squish millipedes and run them on their fur to protect them from mosquitoes!

FIERCE FELINE

Jaguars are good swimmers and have strong legs for climbing. They can weigh about 220 pounds and are expert hunters.

LIANA'S STRONG HOLD

Lianas are wood-stemmed rainforest vines. They wrap around trees growing upward to the sun and canopy. Eventually, the vines strangle the tree.

SHREDDERS

Piranhas are vicious, and they can shred their prey apart in minutes. Piranhas do the most damage in large groups. Piranhas' teeth are so sharp that some people in the Amazon use their jaws as scissors.

HAIRY HUNTER

Tarantulas can grow to be 11 inches long, and their fangs can grow up to 1 inch long. When they get too big for their burrows, they move out and either dig a new burrow or find an empty one to occupy.

THE HARPY

Harpy eagles live in the emergent, or top layer of the rainforest. From there, they see their prey below. They dive down and capture their prey, such as sloths and monkeys. The harpy eagle is the world's most powerful bird of prey.

About the Poems

MINIATURE MONKEY

The pygmy marmoset is the smallest monkey in the world. When pygmy marmosets are born, they are as small as an adult human's pinky finger. When they are full grown, pygmy marmosets can fit into the palm of an adult human's hand. Even though they are small, they eat foods larger than themselves, such as katydids and big fruits.

COATIMUNDI

The coatimundi's tail is used for balance and signaling. Coatimundis signal to other coatimundis if a predator is coming. Coatimundis also need their tails to balance because they climb trees all day.

THE HIGH LIFE

Orchids are plants called epiphytes. They can live without soil, and soak up their food and water from the air. Orchids get their nutrients from dead plants around their roots.

GEMS OF THE RAINFOREST

Poison dart frogs are one of the most poisonous animals in the world, and for good reason, too! The poison from just the frog's skin can kill 100,000 people.

KATY-DID, KATY-DIDN'T

Katydids are extremely colorful. They can be all different colors such as pink, blue, green, and yellow. Katydids blend in with their surroundings. Some katydids can look like green leaves!

MAJESTIC BIRD

The toucan's bill has bright colors. It's a very useful tool. Toucans can use their bill to scare off enemies and to pluck fruit from trees.

ESCAPE ARTIST

Spider monkeys can use their tails to swing from vine to vine and branch to branch. They eat fruits and nuts, and sometimes even bark or honey. The oldest known age of a wild spider monkey is 33 years old.

SLUGGISH SLOTH

Sloths are VERY slow mammals. How slow are sloths? It takes them one minute to go 6 feet! Their fur is so wet, green algae grows on it. The algae in their fur attracts algae-eating bugs such as moths, ticks, and fleas. Sloths live mostly in trees, and they are awake only 8 hours a day!

BUG EATERS

Pitcher plants have a scent that attracts bugs. The bugs then land on the rim of the pitcher and fall into a liquid. Once the bugs fall in, they become drowsy and drown inside the liquid. The plant then digests the bug.

SCALY SKIN

The caiman have very sharp teeth and claws. They lunge at their prey and are very strong. Some caimans can be more than 20 feet long. They spin their bodies in the water to tear off bite-sized chunks from their prey.

TAMARINS

Tamarins sometimes eat out of bromeliad plants. They use their long, thin fingers to snatch out prey such as katydids and lizards.

PREDATORS

The red-eyed tree frog's favorite foods are moths, spiders, flies, and small grasshoppers. When the tree frog is frightened, it darkens its skin color. It bulges its red eyes to scare away predators.

Kids Are Authors®
Books written by children for children

The Kids Are Authors® Competition was established in 1986 to encourage children to read and to become involved in the creative process of writing.

Since then, thousands of children have written and illustrated books as participants in the Kids Are Authors® Competition.

The winning books in the annual competition are published by Scholastic Inc.
and are distributed by Scholastic Book Fairs throughout the United States.

For more information:
Kids Are Authors® 1080 Greenwood Blvd.; Lake Mary, FL 32746
Or visit our web site at: www.scholastic.com/kidsareauthors

All rights reserved. No part of this publication may be reproduced, or stored in a retrieval system, or transmitted in any form or by any means, electronic, mechanical, photocopying, recording, or otherwise, without written permission of the publisher.

For information regarding permission, write to Scholastic Inc.,
Attention: Permission Department, 557 Broadway; New York, NY 10012.

Copyright © 2009 by Scholastic Inc.

Scholastic and associated logos are trademarks and/or
registered trademarks of Scholastic Inc.

ISBN 10: 0-545-21330-4

ISBN 13: 978-0-545-21330-1

12 11 10 9 8 7 6 5 4 3 2 1

Cover and Design by Bill Henderson

Printed and bound in the U.S.A.
First Printing, July 2009

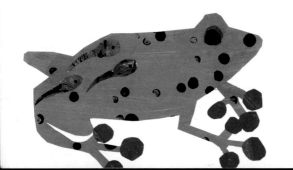